Contents

What is a screenplay?   4

All sorts of screenplays   6

What's your story?   10

The screenplay   14

Who and where?   18

It's all talk   22

The best!   26

First steps to success   28

Glossary   30

Find out more   31

Index   32

Some words are printed in bold, **like this**. You can find out what they mean by looking in the glossary on page 30.

What is a screenplay?

Most television programmes and movies start life as a screenplay or script. Whether it is for television or film, the actors need to know what the characters they are playing will say and do. Similarly, the **director** and other members of the team need instructions. For example, the director needs to know where a movie is located.

What's in a screenplay?

A screenplay includes:

- character descriptions
- **locations** – countries or rooms
- **dialogue** – what characters say, or even the noises they make
- acting and camera directions
- **special effects** – such as explosions or car chases
- sound effects/music.

Here are the stars of *High School Musical 3*. The screenplay for this movie also includes songs.

CULTURE IN ACTION

Writing a Screenplay

Liz Miles

www.raintreepublishers.co.uk
Visit our website to find out more information about Raintree books.

To order:
☎ Phone 0845 6044371
🖹 Fax +44 (0) 1865 312263
🖥 Email myorders@raintreepublishers.co.uk

Customers from outside the UK please telephone +44 1865 312262

Raintree is an imprint of Capstone Global Library Limited, a company incorporated in England and Wales having its registered office at 7 Pilgrim Street, London, EC4V 6LB – Registered company number: 6695582

Edited by Louise Galpine, Rachel Howells, and Helen Cox
Designed by Kimberly Miracle and Betsy Wernert
Original illustrations © Capstone Global Library Ltd
Illustrated by kja-artists.com
Picture research by Mica Brancic and Kay Altwegg
Production by Alison Parsons
Originated by Steve Walker, Capstone Global Library Ltd
Printed in China by Leo Paper Products Ltd

ISBN 978 1 406212 14 3 (hardback)
13 12 11 10 09
10 9 8 7 6 5 4 3 2 1

ISBN 978 1 406212 34 1 (paperback)
14 13 12 11 10
10 9 8 7 6 5 4 3 2 1

British Library Cataloguing in Publication Data
Miles, Liz
Writing a screenplay. – (Culture in action)
791.4'375
A full catalogue record for this book is available from the British Library.

Acknowledgements

We would like to thank the following for permission to reproduce photographs: Alamy p. **28** (Jim West); Getty Images pp. **18** (Michael Ochs Archives), **26** (Vince Bucci); Rex Features pp. **4** (Everett/© W. Disney), **6** (Everett/© 20th Century Fox), **7** (Everett Collection), **8** (Humberto Carreno), **9** (Everett Collection), **19** (Everett/© 20th Century Fox), **20** (Everett/W. Disney), **21** (Everett Collection), **27** (Everett/ © BuenaVista), **29** (David Fisher); The Kobal Collection pp. **5** (Jonathan Wenk), **10** (Nickelodeon Movies), **11** (Warner Bros/DC Comics), **12** (20th Century Fox), **15** (Universal Studios/Sophie Giraud), **16** (Universal/Richard Cartwright), **22** (Castle Rock/Shangri-La Entertainment), **23** (Universal City Studios/Rhythm & Blues).

Icon and banner images supplied by Shutterstock: © Alexander Lukin, © ornitopter, © Colorlife, and © David S. Rose.

Cover photograph of a still from the film *Journey to the Center of the Earth* reproduced with permission of The Kobal Collection (New Line Cinema).

We would like to thank George Zwierzynski Jr., Jackie Murphy, and Nancy Harris for their invaluable help in the preparation of this book.

Every effort has been made to contact copyright holders of material reproduced in this book. Any omissions will be rectified in subsequent printings if notice is given to the publishers.

Screenwriter David Koepp is said to have earned $4 million for writing just one screenplay.

The root of the idea

The people who write screenplays are called screenwriters. A screenwriter starts with an idea. The idea may be original. Television **soaps**, for example, are usually based on a new idea. Many screenplays are an **adaptation** – they are based on a work that already exists, such as a comic book or a novel. Many scripts are the result of collaboration. Collaboration is when a team of writers work together to write and revise a script.

Guess who?

Even the best screenwriters often go unnoticed. For example, you may know of such films as *Jurassic Park* (1993) and *Spider-Man* (2002), but do you know who wrote the scripts? In fact, David Koepp wrote the scripts. He is a very successful US screenwriter.

5

All sorts of screenplays

A vast range of screenplays are written for the worlds of film and television. Each type of screenplay needs different writing skills and is targeted at a different audience. They vary from long movies about disasters for adults, such as *Titanic* (1997), to funny cartoon series for children, such as *Scooby Doo*.

The audience and the **budget** for a movie may be much bigger than for a television programme. This means that a film screenwriter can include more costly actors and **locations** than the writer of a cheaper television series.

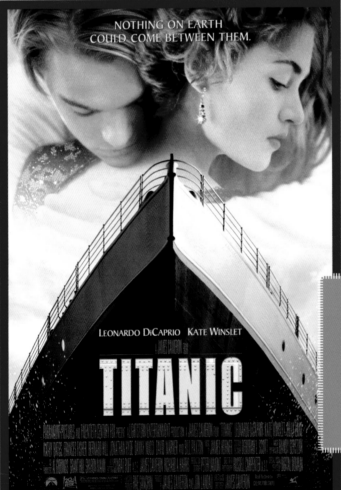

Titanic had a big budget of $200 million. This meant that the screenwriter could include lots of scenes that were expensive to make.

Some television programmes last for years. The first series of *Scooby Doo* was shown in 1969!

A series or one-off?

A series of films is a number of movies that have similar characters and/or settings. Each of the movies has a complete story and stands alone. An example of this is the *Spider-Man* series of films.

A series for television is a run of programmes, called episodes, that follow lengthy **plots**. In some series, such as **soaps**, the screenwriters have to include **cliff-hangers** at the end of each episode. They hope that an exciting ending will make the audience want to watch the next episode. A soap can last for many years. *Coronation Street*, for example, began in 1960.

Doctor Popular

The final episode of the fourth series of the new *Doctor Who* in July 2008 had 9.4 million viewers. Its Christmas special in 2007 had done even better. It was watched by 12.2 million viewers!

Original or adaptation?

Screenplays can be original work or **adaptations**. An original screenplay is based on a new idea. An adaptation is based on already-published material, which can range from a novel to a comic. How close an adaptation is to the published material varies. For example, some fans of the Harry Potter books complain about the changes they have spotted in the film adaptations.

From page to screen

To change a novel into a screenplay is a complicated job. Everything that happens has to come through **dialogue** and visual action. One screenwriting rule is "Show it, don't say it". There is rarely a narrator's voice to tell you what is happening or what people are thinking.

Lasting characters

Screenplays are often based on interesting characters that were invented in the past. Several screenplays for film have been written about Batman and Spider-Man. These characters first appeared in comics, in 1939 and 1962.

This shot is from *Spider-Man 3* (2007). The superhero appears in lots of screenplays – for movies, TV action series, and animated cartoons.

New characters are often created for an original film and become hugely popular. The comical characters of Wallace and Gromit first appeared in a short film in 1989 called *A Grand Day Out*. At least five more screenplays have since been written, featuring the same man and dog.

Period dramas

Classic novels are often adapted into period dramas for television and film. (A period drama is a story set in the past.) Screenwriters who adapt a novel, such as Jane Austen's *Pride and Prejudice*, must update dialogue that was written nearly 200 years ago for today's audiences to enjoy.

This period drama is an adaptation of a book. The television series has the same title: *Pride and Prejudice*. The book was written nearly 200 years ago.

What's your story?

The most important part of a script is the **plot**, or story. A good plot captures the audience's interest from the start. It then holds its attention to the end.

The essentials

A good plot should include:

- Characters and setting: The main character or characters should be introduced early on. The screenwriter must make the viewer care about what happens to them, and what they will do. The setting must be believable enough to seem real.

- Problem: A problem for the main character should appear early on. It is the "dramatic conflict" that provides the drama, or action. It pushes the character into action, to seek an answer.

- Climax: The character struggles to find a solution until the end – it could be a showdown, a car chase, or a battle.

- The resolution: The answer to the problem provides the ending. It should be believable and satisfying for the audience.

In *The Spiderwick Chronicles* (2008) the problem is a book that brings goblins to life. The climax is a battle with goblins.

Superman Returns (2006) uses a flashback to tell the back story of how the hero first realized he could fly.

Back story

A plot covers a specific time span and often starts at a certain point in a character's life. **Back story** is made up of the events that have come before. For example, Batman's back story is how he witnessed the murder of his parents, and grew up determined to fight crime.

Back story sometimes appears through flashbacks, dream sequences, or **dialogue**. However, too much back story can bore the audience.

Subplots

A subplot is a less important story that happens alongside the main story. There can be more than one. A subplot can provide depth, variety, or extra action. In *Batman* movies, any romance in the superhero's life provides a change from all the action.

Series plotting

A television series, such as a **soap**, needs lots of dramatic conflicts that run together. Each conflict has to be resolved in a different episode. This holds the audience's interest over weeks, or even months. Screenplays that have several plots need a team of 10 or more writers.

Cliff-hangers can draw vast audiences. In the television series *Dallas* (1980), a character called JR was injured. "Who shot JR?" was discussed in many newspapers and chat shows.

Comedy

The drama in a comedy plot comes from characters' shock, surprise, bewilderment, and awkwardness. Often, the humour is in seeing adults behave like children. In *Home Alone* (1990), for example, the bumbling burglars who try to invade Kevin's home while his parents are away on holiday are very child-like.

In *Home Alone*, the long screams from 8-year-old Kevin make the audience laugh rather than shake with fear.

Setting the mood

A screenplay may include ideas for **incidental music** or music for the beginning of the film or programme. The music may have an important connection to the subject of the film, or the **lyrics** might provide information the writer wants the audience to hear.

Imagine you are a screenwriter for a television series. You have been asked to find a new theme tune. A theme tune is a tune played at the start and end of the programme.

Steps to follow:

1. Choose from:

   a) a **sitcom**, such as *Friends*

   b) a **sci-fi** (science fiction) series, such as *Doctor Who*

   c) a series of your own invention.

2. Hunt for a section of music that would suit the mood – funny, sad, or frightening.

Listen to a range of music, such as classical or pop, to decide on a tune that is memorable. This will help the viewer recognize the television series when the music starts.

3. Think about the following during your search:

   a) How do you want the listener to feel when they hear the music?

   b) Do you want your music to appeal to adults or children, or both?

4. Play your choices to friends, and then discuss them. Describe the type of music you have chosen, and why.

The screenplay

There are many different parts to a screenplay and all are laid out in a certain way. This makes it easy for **directors**, actors, actresses, and others to find what they are looking for quickly. Straightaway, they can see which is the **dialogue** and which is a direction. Each page of a screenplay is usually equal to around one minute of screen time when the film or programme is finished.

1

112 EXT – DAY

(The entrance to a cave. ELLA and ADAM walking into cave. Ella looking at a map.)

ELLA **6**

This way. This is the cave.

CUT TO: **4**

8 113 INT – DARK CAVE

(The camera is watching a flickering green light coming towards the characters or camera from the back of the cave. A rustling coming from the light, getting louder.) **5**

ADAM tugs at ELLA's arm. **2**

ADAM

(whispers)

Come on! Let's get out of here!

ELLA

(crossly)

No. We're not going anywhere. **7**

We've got to stay and see him.

To ask our question.

3 (Close-up. The light shows the characters' faces. They are staring up at the source of the light.)

ADAM

(scared)

Its eyes. Look at its eyes!

(Tilt to show face of DRAGON, light beams from its bloodshot eyes, staring down at the characters.)

ELLA

Shhh. Don't talk like that. You'll upset him.

(Ella talks nervously, politely to DRAGON)

Sir, please can you help us?

1. *Scene description:* Shows where the scene is set and whether it is an interior (INT) or exterior (EXT) scene. It usually tells you if the scene is set during the day or night.

2. *Action description:* Describes the action of the scene and what the characters do.

3. *Camera instructions:* If a certain camera move or angle is essential to the **plot**, it should be included.

4. *"Fade in" and "cut to":* Instruct how softly or dramatically one scene should change to the next.

5. *Sound directions:* Special sounds or noises may be essential to the plot. Some are written in capital letters to show their importance.

6. *Character speaking:* The name of the character speaking.

7. *Dialogue:* The dialogue is all the words that the performers speak. The dialogue is indented (nearer the middle of the page) so that it is easy to find and follow. There may be instructions in brackets or *italic* type to describe how the words should be spoken.

8. *Scene number:* Makes it easy to find a certain place in the screenplay. Scenes are often rehearsed and filmed out of order. For example, all indoor scenes may be done first if a **location** has been rented for a few days.

Each scene filmed for a movie starts with the "clack" of a clapperboard. The information on the board and its "clack" are used to put all the scenes and sound recordings together later.

Stories in pictures

Visualising a story is vital when writing a successful screenplay. You need to imagine how each scene will look as it is filmed. For example, a crowded outdoor scene, such as a battle, would need a wide-angle shot from the camera. A wide-angle means a wide area is seen in one go.

Camera directions often used are:

- Point of view (POV): A shot as if seen from a character's point of view
- Close-up (CU): Shows detail, such as a character's face
- Pull back (PB): When the camera pulls back, more of the scene comes into view
- Cut to: This is a clean break from one scene to another
- Fade out: The scene goes black.
- Fade in: A new scene comes out of the black.
- Dissolve: From one scene to another, without going to black.

Storyboard

Directors or screenwriters often sketch out a **storyboard** to help them. They draw each camera shot, showing what the camera sees, and even its angle. For example, if the camera is seeing what a mouse sees, it might be angled up from the floor.

This is a storyboard for a scary movie.

Camera eyes

Steps to follow:

1. Choose a simple short story (or write your own). Imagine you are planning a television **adaptation** of it.

2. Plan and draw a storyboard of five to ten pictures. Pick the most important scenes for each picture. Remember to include the problem, or dramatic conflict, and resolution. What should be the focus for each scene? Will your picture show a close-up or a wide-angle view? Will it be from a character's point of view?

3. When you have finished the pictures, write a caption for each. Together, the captions will briefly tell the story.

Consider what the focus should be for each scene. For example, which character is the most important?

Here is an example of a well-known story, written in five captions:

1. Cinderella cannot go to the ball. (Dramatic conflict.)

2. A fairy godmother waves her wand.

3. The prince dances with Cinderella.

4. Cinderella leaves her slipper behind.

5. The slipper fits Cinderella. (Final resolution.)

Who and where?

As we have seen, it is a main character's struggle that provides the dramatic action in a **plot**. This means that creating a character who is likely to face problems is a first step in writing a screenplay. The second step is thinking of a **location** or situation. A location can provide the character with the necessary problems.

Comedy characters

Comic characters have been popular since the early days of cinema. Some of the earliest comedies focused on clownish characters. Charlie Chaplain's character "the Tramp" (a tramp is a homeless person) in the early 1900s was popular because people both laughed at and felt sorry for him.

The Tramp (middle) is always getting into trouble. He is a silly and child-like comedy character.

Characters in comedy are always facing problems. The adults are usually childish. They struggle with a world that is filled with possible disasters. For example, when a comedy character steps in a puddle, the puddle might turn out to be a deep muddy hole.

The cast

Screenwriters supply a list of all the characters. Actors and actresses usually read a script before accepting a part in a movie or programme.

How to create a character

To create a convincing character you need to know every detail about them. They need to be well-rounded and believable. Ask and answer lots of questions about the character! For example, what colour is his/her hair? What books does he/she like to read? What would your character do if . . . ?

This is a comic scene from *The Simpsons Movie* (2007). Every member of the Simpson family has a quirky character.

A hungry rat in a kitchen leads to lots of trouble (and comedy) in *Ratatouille*.

Setting the scene

The location of a story is a vital part of it. Different locations add drama, atmosphere (the feeling of a place), variety, and comedy. A screenplay may include instructions, such as "Thick fog covers the forest path ahead".

From sitting rooms to outer space

The setting must suit the **genre**. Television **soaps** and **sitcoms** are usually set in everyday locations. This helps the viewers to understand the problems the characters face. In contrast, a **sci-fi** drama needs a stranger setting, such as an alien planet.

Specific locations give the writer all sorts of opportunities for things to happen to the characters. The restaurant kitchen location in *Ratatouille* (2007) leads to lots of comic events with food.

Mood changes

A change of location adds to the drama or suspense. When the main character, Lyra, goes to the Arctic in *The Golden Compass* (2007), the bleak atmosphere adds to the suspense. If heroes or heroines are put in dangerous places, we worry about them more. Seeing a character wrestle close to a cliff-edge is more worrying than seeing them wrestle on a sofa.

How much does it cost?

Of course, the choice of location affects the cost of a film or television programme. Although **special effects** mean that just about any location is possible, far-out locations are very expensive. Usually, television programmes have to cost less than movies. This means that television scripts are often set in everyday locations, or that far-out locations are faked on a studio set.

Characters in *The Golden Compass* struggle to survive in the Arctic. The cold, bleak setting adds to the tension.

It's all talk

Dialogue is all the spoken words from characters in a film or fictional television programme. The writer uses dialogue to reveal the characters, move the story along, and provide information.

Choice of words

The words a character uses can reveal a lot. Using long words might suggest they are well-educated. Lots of slang (casual words) might suggest they are streetwise. "Snot" and "manky" are slang words.

There isn't a lot of dialogue in *The Polar Express*, but nearly every sentence tells us something important.

How characters interact

How characters talk also tells us a lot. In *The Polar Express* (2004), one boy is very quiet. He is not excited about Christmas and doesn't want to see Santa. He wants to be alone, saying to the others: "Christmas just doesn't work out for me. Never has."

The replies from the boy and girl show they feel sorry for him, and show they are kind and caring: "But Christmas is such a wonderful, beautiful time." "… this is Christmas Eve. Don't stay here by yourself." "We'll go together."

Back story and plot

Because there is usually no narrator to tell us what has happened or is going to happen, the dialogue needs to keep the **plot** moving. The movie *Harry Potter and the Chamber of Secrets* (2002) opens with a visit from an elf named Dobby, who tells Harry: "Harry Potter must not go back to Hogwarts School of Witchcraft and Wizardry this year." This is **back story** (see page 11). It tells us that Harry has been to this school already. Dobby then moves the plot along: "If Harry Potter goes back to school he will be in great danger." We now know that Harry Potter is going to be in danger because we are pretty sure he *will* go back to school!

In screenplays, words can come from the mouths of anyone or anything: elves, giants, or mermaids! In *Babe* (1995), the "star" pig says lots of funny things.

Subtext

Often, there is an important meaning or feeling behind what a character says. This is called the subtext. Sometimes, a character can say one thing but mean something quite different. The character might avoid a subject altogether. Sometimes what characters don't say (the subtext) is more telling than what they do say.

JAMAL
Wow! We can make money.
Lots! Just think! A talking duck!
This is going to make us rich!
ANNA
People won't believe it.
Dad won't believe a duck can speak.
Anyway, he hates ducks.
JAMAL
Oh come on. Let's try.
This duck is brilliant at telling jokes.
He'll make us famous. We'll be rich!
ANNA
(turns to Dave, the duck)
I'm not sure. Dave, what do you think?
DAVE, THE DUCK
Sure. I can make us rich!
I'd get lots of laughs. But just one thing …
some people eat ducks, don't they?
JAMAL
No one will eat a funny duck!
You'll be the safest duck in the world. A star.
So let's sell tickets for a show on Saturday.
We'll put up posters. Dave, you'd better
start rehearsing.

Reveals character:
Short phrases show a character's excitement or fear

Reveals character:
This shows what the character thinks of the situation

Information:
This gives us extra details about the situation

Back story:
Background information is important for this plot

Subtext:
Although the words suggest the character is brave, the pause suggests he is just trying to be brave, when in fact he is scared

Plot:
A sentence like this moves the story along

PERFORMANCE ACTIVITY

Camera rolling

Write and perform your own script. You can work alone by writing a **monologue**. A monologue is one person talking or thinking out loud. If you want to work with friends, write a scene for two or three characters, using dialogue. Dialogue is all the words that characters speak.

You could choose from the following:

- A lonely animal is planning an escape from a zoo (monologue in an animated movie)

- A young explorer has discovered a dragon in a cave (dialogue for a fantasy adventure movie)

- A school girl or boy is late getting home and must explain why to his or her parents (dialogue for a **soap**).

Plan your script by thinking about these questions:

- What is the plot? What is the back story?

- What are the characters like? How are they feeling?

- What do the characters want to happen next? Will anything they say or do change things?

- What will you make happen next?

Keep your dialogue short and simple, especially for dramatic scenes such as this!

Read your script out loud as you write it. Does it sound natural? When acting your script try different expressions and tones of voice.

The best!

Screenwriters are often unknown. It is the **directors**, actors, and actresses who get all the attention. However, a few screenwriters have become better known, such as Mike Leigh and Woody Allen. This is partly because they are successful directors too!

It is hard to become a successful screenwriter. Film and television companies tend to rely on the writers they already know for blockbuster films or big **budget** dramas.

Here are some of the great screenwriters who have succeeded:

Peter Jackson

Jackson is a film director, producer (person who organises the money needed to make a movie), and screenwriter. He worked on the *Lord of the Rings* trilogy (2001–03) and *King Kong* (2005).

Brad Bird

Many screenwriters are multi-talented. Brad Bird is an Oscar-winning director, plus screenwriter and actor in *The Incredibles* (2004) and *Ratatouille* (2007).

Diablo Cody is an American screenwriter. She won an Oscar for best screenplay for *Juno* (2007).

The funny and exciting screenplays for the *Pirates of the Caribbean* movies were a team effort – written by two men called Terry and Ted.

Terry and Ted

Screenwriters often work in pairs, such as Terry Rossio and Ted Elliott. Together, they wrote the screenplay for *Aladdin* (1992) and the *Pirates of the Caribbean* films.

Andrew Davies

Davies is one of the best-known television screenwriters. He is admired for his **adaptations** of novels that were written in the past, such as *Pride and Prejudice* by Jane Austen. He adapts the stories so that modern audiences can easily enjoy them.

Adele Rose

Adele Rose is an example of a hard-working and successful screenwriter who is not well known by the public. Hundreds of writers are involved in creating a long-running **soap opera**, such as *Coronation Street*. Adele Rose stands out for writing the most episodes of all – a grand total of 455!

First steps to success

Lots of people hope to follow in the footsteps of some of the big names in screenwriting. An award for a great television series, or an award for best original screenplay, may also be their goal.

First stage

Writing short scenes is a good way to start. Joining a writing group or club, and working with other writers is helpful, too. Practise is essential, as even the most skilled screenwriters rewrite and revise their work over and over again.

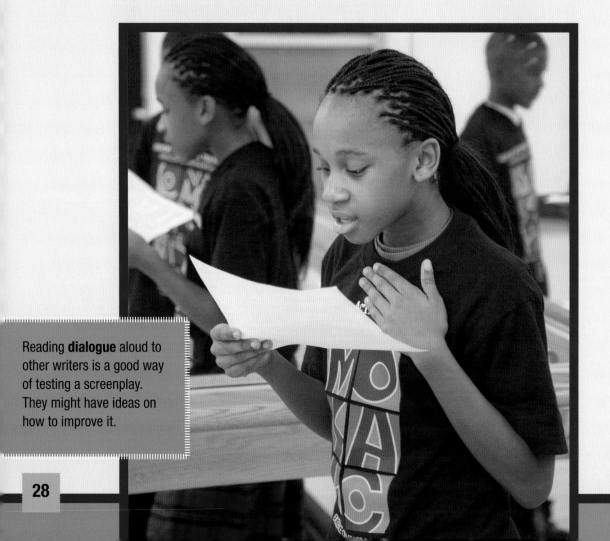

Reading **dialogue** aloud to other writers is a good way of testing a screenplay. They might have ideas on how to improve it.

In 2007, 14-year-old Rosalind Peters won an award for her own film, which she wrote and filmed. It is called *The Unwelcome Stranger*.

Learn from the experts

The only way to find out what makes a script successful is to study scripts by well-known writers. There are plenty of free sources of scripts on the Internet.

How to write for television

People often start writing for television by picking their favourite television series and writing an episode for it. Study the programme first. Note down the characters, how they speak, and their stories so far. Then have a go at writing.

How to write for the movies

Some top movie writers (and **directors**), such as Peter Jackson, found success by making their own short film. It is fairly easy to make a movie. You can use a digital video-recorder, **video-editing program**, and computer. Even if the final movie is not perfect, it will show how good or bad the screenplay is. At least you will find out what needs to be improved.

Glossary

adaptation screenplay that is based on already published material. Shakespeare's plays are often adapted for television.

back story events that have come before the time the story takes place

budget available money. A multimillion pound budget is common in the movie world, but rare for television programmes.

cliff-hanger high point of suspense at the end of a television episode or series. A good cliff-hanger makes an audience want to watch the next episode.

dialogue words that the actors speak

director person that controls how a film or TV programme is made. The director tells the actors how each scene should be acted.

genre film or programme that has a certain type of content and form. Action is a genre that has lots of special effects.

incidental music music that accompanies action or dialogue. Creepy incidental music adds suspense to a horror film.

location where movie or TV programmes are filmed. "On location" means that the filming is done outside the studio.

lyrics words sung to music

monologue one person talking or thinking out loud

plot main events in a story, film, or TV programme. A plot needs a clear beginning or problem, and a clear end or resolution.

sci-fi (short for science fiction) any story that is to do with the future or outer space. Sci-fi movies are often set in the future, or involve space ships and aliens.

sitcom situation-comedy series that puts everyday people in embarrassing or humorous situations. *Friends* is one of the most popular American sitcoms ever made.

soap or **soap opera** series of episodes about fictional people and their everyday lives. Soap operas involve teams of screenwriters, who write the many plots for numerous episodes.

special effects any events, characters, or settings that need stunts or computer-generated images. For example, the way a giant gorilla appears to jump over a burning building is achieved using special effects.

storyboard sequence of images to show how scenes should look when they are filmed. Storyboards for animations show some of the pictures the animators will have to draw.

video-editing program computer software that helps you alter a film you have made. You can use this type of program to change the order of scenes and to add music or sounds.

Find out more

Books

Write for Success (Life Skills), Jim Mack (Heinemann Library, 2009)

Write that Film Script (Get Writing!), Shaun McCarthy (Heinemann Library, 2004)

Write that Play (Get Writing!), Shaun McCarthy (Heinemann Library, 2004)

Websites

www.bbc.co.uk/cbbc/meandmymovie
Watch other children's films or upload your own at this website.

www.filmstreet.co.uk
Search the library on adaptations, or submit a video of your own screenplay!

Places to visit

BFI IMAX Cinema
1 Charlie Chaplin Walk
South Bank
Waterloo
London
SE1 8XR
Tel: +44 (0)20 7928 3232
www.bfi.org.uk

See some of the best movies and TV programmes on the biggest screen in the UK.

You could also ask your school if they can book a visit from a writer who will give you some tips in person, or contact your local library to ask if they have any creative writing workshops.

Index

acting directions 4
action descriptions 15
actors and actresses 4, 6, 14, 19, 26
Allen, Woody 26

Babe 23
back story 11, 23, 24
Batman 8, 11
Bird, Brad 26
budgets 6, 26

camera directions 4, 15, 16
  close-up (CU) 16
  cut to 15, 16
  dissolve 16
  fade out/fade in 15, 16
  point of view (POV) 16
  pull back (PB) 16
Chaplin, Charlie 18
characters 8–9, 10, 24, 25
  character descriptions 4
  comic 18–19
  creating 19
clapperboards 15
cliff-hangers 7, 12
Cody, Diablo 26
collaboration 5, 12, 27
comic characters 18–19
comic plots 12, 20
Coronation Street 7, 27

Dallas 12
Davies, Andrew 27
dialogue 4, 8, 11, 15, 22–25, 28
  choice of words 22
  monologues 25
  slang 22
  subtext 24

directors 4, 14, 16, 26
Doctor Who 7
dramatic conflicts 10, 12, 17, 19

Elliott, Ted 27
exposition 11

film series 7

genres 20
Golden Compass, The 21

Harry Potter adaptations 8, 23
Home Alone 12
home movie-making 29

Jackson, Peter 26, 29

Koepp, David 5

Leigh, Mike 26
locations 4, 6, 10, 15, 18, 20–21
  changes of 21
  faking 21

monologues 25
music 4, 13
  incidental music 13
  lyrics 13
  theme tunes 13

novels 8
  adaptations 5, 8, 9, 27

period dramas 9
Pirates of the Caribbean 27
plots 7, 10, 18, 23, 24, 25
  back story 11, 23, 24
  comedy plots 12, 20
  ingredients 10
  subplots 11

Polar Express, The 22

Ratatouille 20, 26
resolutions 10, 17
Rose, Adele 27
Rossio, Terry 27

scene descriptions 15
scene numbers 15
sci-fi dramas 20
Scooby Doo 6, 7
screenplays
  adaptations 5, 8, 9, 17, 27
  items included in 4, 15
  original screenplays 8
screenwriters 5
  becoming a screenwriter 28–29
  collaboration 5, 12, 27
  successful 26–27
scripts, free sources of 29
Simpsons, The 19
situation comedies 20
soaps 5, 7, 12, 20, 25, 27
sound effects 4, 15
special effects 4, 21
Spider-Man 5, 7, 8
storyboards 16, 17
subplots 11
subtext 24
Superman series 11

television series 6, 7, 12, 21, 29
Titanic 6

visualising a story 16

Wallace and Gromit 9